THERE'S A LOT MORE THAN PRETTY WINDMILLS IN POLAND!

GEOGRAPHY BOOKS FOR THIRD GRADE CHILDREN'S EUROPE BOOKS

BABY PROFESSOR
EDUCATION KIDS

Speedy Publishing LLC

40 E. Main St. #1156

Newark, DE 19711

www.speedypublishing.com

Copyright 2017

In this book, we're going to talk about exploring the country of **POLAND**.
So, let's get right to it!

WHERE IS POLAND?

The country of Poland is in the center of Europe. Its northern border is a coastline along the Baltic Sea. The Carpathian Mountains are in the southern region of the country. The country of Germany is to the west of Poland. Bordering Poland at its southern end from west to east are the Czech Republic, Slovakia, and the Ukraine.

Its northeastern border is shared with Russian Kaliningrad, Lithuania, and Belarus. Over 38 million people live in Poland and its landmass is a little smaller than the state of New Mexico.

WHAT ARE THE GEOGRAPHIC AND NATURAL FEATURES OF POLAND?

Most of the terrain of Poland can be described as lowland plains. However, in the north, there are dense areas of forest around the region known as Mazury. This section of the country has over 2,000 glacial lakes as well as 200 kilometers of canals.

MAZURY LAKE

BIALOWIEZA FOREST

The only remaining lowland forest in Europe is in Poland. This forest is Bialowieza Forest. It's the largest area that still has the type of primeval forest that used to cover most of Europe during prehistoric times. It is in the eastern region of Poland at the border of Poland and Belarus. You can only access it by foot or by traveling in a horse-drawn carriage.

There is a rare European bison, called a wisent, living in the Bialowieza Forest. At one time this huge mammal was extinct in the wild. Scientists bred the animals in captivity and released them back into the wild. Now they are thriving in the forest, which has the world's largest population of wisents.

BEAR

The expansive forests in Poland are also home to brown bears, wild boar, chamois goats, wild horses, red deer, roe deer, and Eurasian lynxes.

The country of Poland has the largest number of gray wolves in Europe.

Poland has had many wars in its history. These conflicts, in addition to industrial pollution, have taken their toll on the land. There has been a long tradition of protection of nature so the government is doing its best to restore plant and animal habitats.

GRAY WOLF

BOLECHOWICKI GULLY NATURE RESERVE

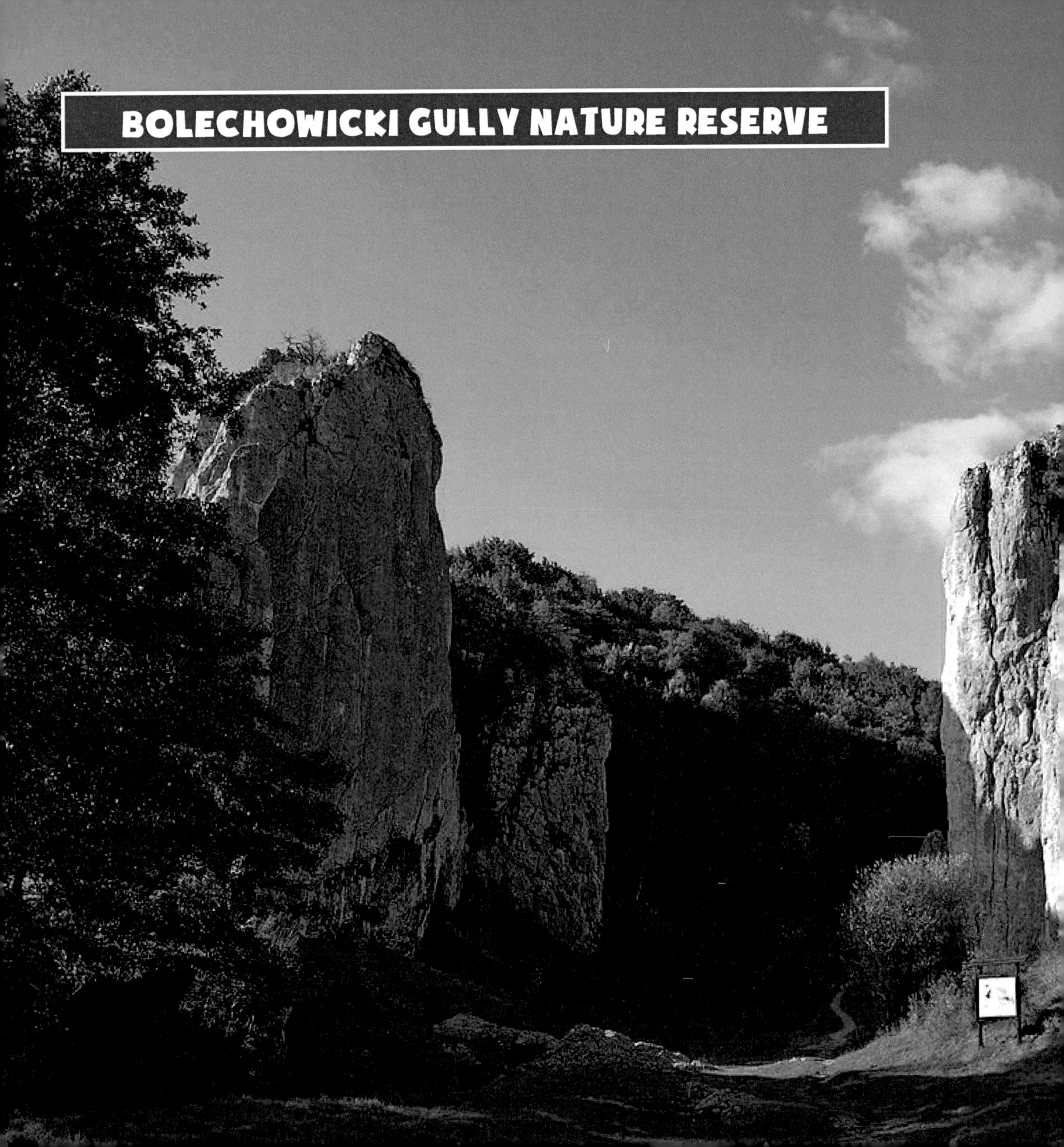

The leaders of the country want to ensure that future generations will see the beautiful plant and animal life in Poland. There are over 20 national parks, a hundred sanctuaries for birds, and over 1,200 nature reserves in the country.

WHAT IS THE CULTURE LIKE IN POLAND?

Religion is very important to the Polish people. Most of the population is Roman Catholic. Although most popes have been from Italy, in 1978, Cardinal Karol Wojtyla, who was the archbishop of the city of Krakow, was voted by the cardinals in Rome to become the first pope from Poland. He was the first non-Italian pope in 400 years.

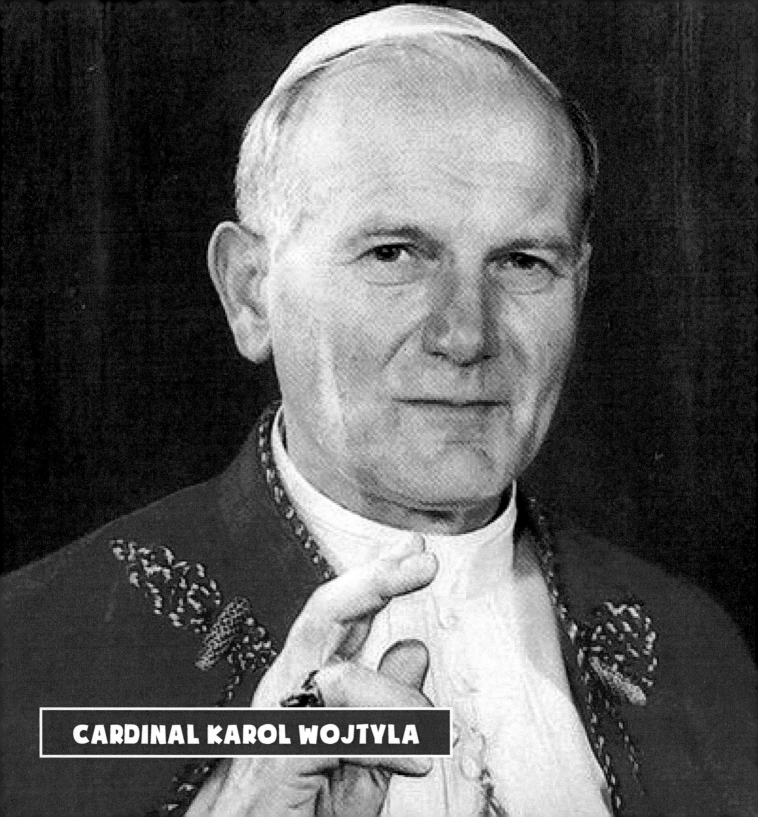

CARDINAL KAROL WOJTYLA

His papal name was John Paul II and he was the leader of the Roman Catholic Church until he passed away in 2005. He was declared a saint in 2014. Pope John Paul II played an important role in the rise of Solidarity in Poland and the collapse of the Soviet Union.

WHAT IS THE HISTORY OF POLAND?

The first civilization in the country dates back to around 2000 B.C. In the 1500s, the countries of Lithuania and Poland united to form a large kingdom. Two hundred years later, Poland's government was weakened by a series of wars. In 1795, the countries of Austria, Russia, and Prussia, which is now modern-day Germany, divided up Poland. It wasn't an independent country for more than 120 years. After World War I, Poland's borders were restored.

However, during the Second World War, Germany and the Soviet Union took over the lands of Poland. After World War II, the Soviets instituted communist rule there. In 1980, there was a very important movement in Poland called "Solidarity." Polish workers began to revolt against communist rule. After almost ten years of protests, democratic elections were held and the communist party was dissolved in Poland.

WHAT PLACES ARE GOOD FOR EXPLORING IN POLAND?

There are so many amazing places to visit in Poland. Here are just a few examples of places you can visit.

THE CITY OF MALBORK

Would you like to pretend that you're living in medieval times? If so, you'll enjoy exploring the castle at Malbork. It is the largest fortress in the Gothic style that exists in Europe. Constructed in the 13th century by the Knights of the Teutonic Order, this beautiful castle was built to be their headquarters. The town of Malbrock is better known by the name "Marienburg."

It was given this German name to honor the Virgin Mary who was the patron saint of both the castle and the city. The castle is really three different castles in one and is the largest castle constructed of brick in the world.

OLD WINDMILL

THE CITY OF SKANSEN

Would you like to take a photograph of a beautiful windmill? There are windmills all over the country of Poland and modern wind power is being used in Poland as well. If you would like to see some of the older historic windmills of Poland and imagine what life was like back then, you should visit Skansen in Dziekanowice.

In Skansen, you can walk among 18th and 19th century buildings that were relocated to the open-air museum from the historic Wielkopolska area. Lake Lednica is nearby. It is a scenic area where young people from all over Poland gather for a prayer meeting in June every year.

THE CITY OF TORUN

Are you a budding astronomer? Then, you might be interested in visiting the city of Torun where the famous astronomer Copernicus was born. Torun is situated on the Vistula River and managed to escape the bombing that many cities suffered during World War II. Because of that, the city has buildings that date back to the Middle Ages, including its Gothic town hall, which has built in the 13th century.

ST. JOHN THE BAPTIST CHURCH

This building is thought to be one of the most beautiful places in the world. There are also Gothic churches, such as the Cathedral of Saint John the Evangelist as well as the Cathedral of St. John the Baptist, that date to the 14th century.

TATRA NATIONAL PARK

Do you like to hike on trails or explore caves? Then, the Tatra National Park in southcentral Poland is someplace you would like to visit. The park is filled with scenic beauty throughout its meadows, dense forests, and rock formations that cover the Tatra mountains. There are over 600 caves to explore.

There are 30 beautiful alpine lakes and a spectacular waterfall called Wielka Siklawa that is 230 feet in height. There are 170 miles of trails to enjoy in this park, which is the most visited park in the country.

WIELKA SIKLAWA

THE CITY OF LUBLIN

Are you interested in ancient history? You might enjoy exploring the city of Lublin. This historic city is east of the Vistula River and is situated on the eastern border of Poland. Some of the ancient buildings that stood there were destroyed by various invaders over the years, but the market place dates back to the sixth century.

Prior to World War II, Lublin was the location of a thriving Jewish community, one of the largest in Poland before the Holocaust. Some buildings show evidence of a mixture of Russian and Byzantine styles, a blend of East and West cultures. The Holy Trinity Chapel is an example of that blended architecture.

HOLY TRINITY CHAPEL

SEAPORT AT GDANSK

THE CITY OF GDANSK

Would you like to stand on the shores of the Baltic Sea? If the answer is yes, Gdansk, also known as Danzig, is a city you might like to visit. It is the largest of Poland's northern cities and is also its main seaport. At times it was a portion of Germany but then became part of Poland again after World War II.

The city was completely rebuilt after the war and its Old Town was brought back to its former glory. The royal road that the ancient Polish kings walked can still be seen in this historic city. The city's shipyards were the birthplace of the important Solidarity movement.

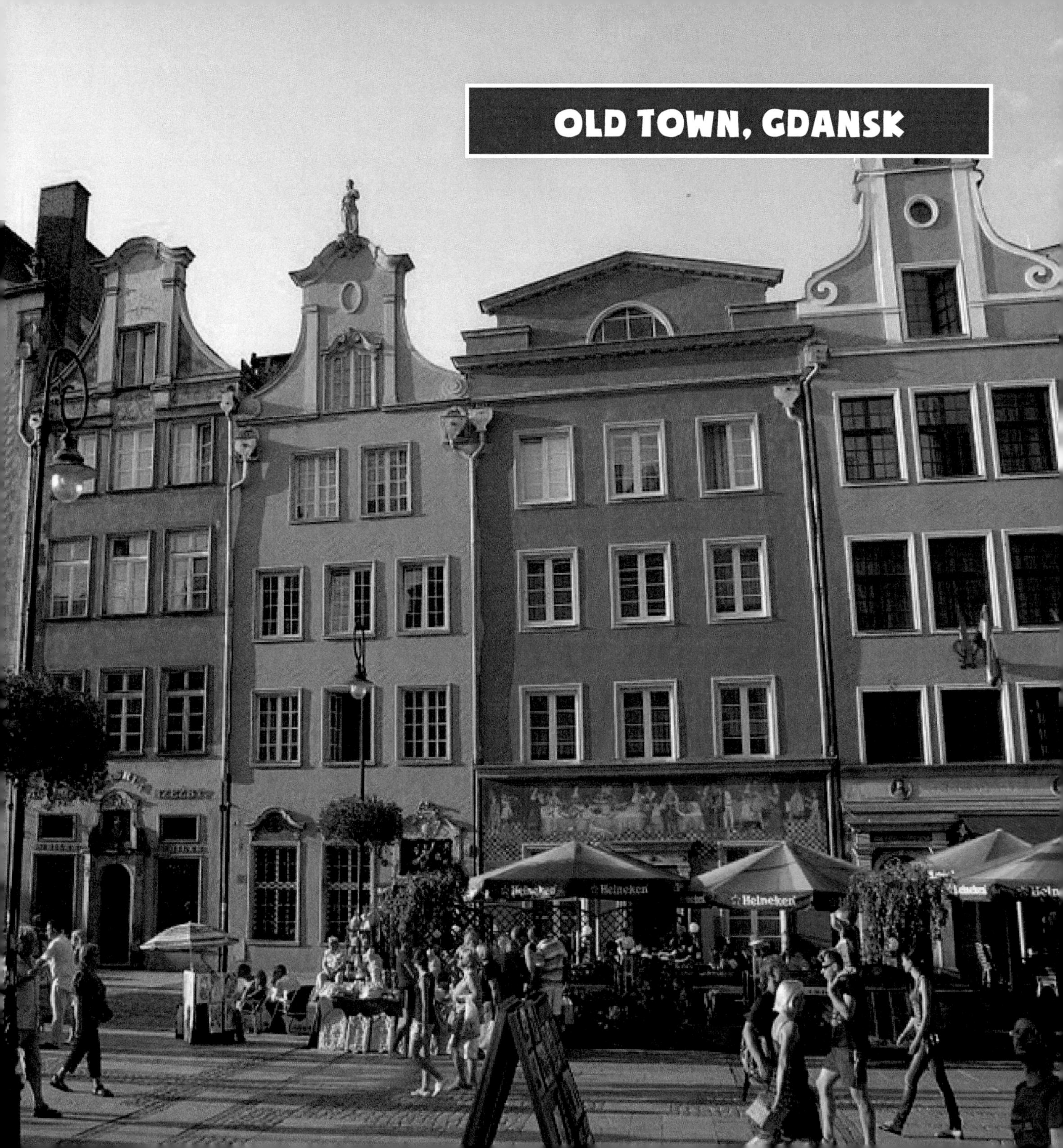

OLD TOWN, GDANSK

GIRAFFE IN WROCLAW ZOO

THE CITY OF WROCLAW

Would you like to see an amazing zoo? Then you might want to visit the city of Wroclaw. Wroclaw is western Poland's largest city and has the largest zoo in the country with animals from all over the world. The city has been part of Poland since after World War II. The zoo isn't the only attraction in the city.

It also has incredible architecture including the Old Town Hall, the market square, and St. Elizabeth's Church, which has a large observation deck that gives you an expansive view of the city.

BEAUTIFUL POLAND!

Poland has had a difficult history and has been fought over and divided many times. Throughout its history, Poland has remained a country of great natural beauty with fiercely proud, religious people. If you visit, you can explore its historic windmills and its gothic architecture. You can learn about its history, walk along trails in its scenic mountains, and encounter a European bison in its primeval forest.

Awesome! Now that you've gone exploring in Poland, you may want to visit the country of Italy in the Baby Professor book *Take Me Back to Italy – Geography Education for Kids.*

Visit

BABY PROFESSOR
EDUCATION KIDS

www.BabyProfessorBooks.com
to download Free Baby Professor eBooks
and view our catalog of new and exciting
Children's Books

Made in the USA
San Bernardino, CA
16 August 2018